Comments on the original Theory is Fun books.

As a music teacher, I have all my children and adults start with this little book. The basics of music theory are laid out succinctly and clearly, with accompanying short exercises.

Dr T J Worrall

I'm a music teacher, and can honestly say this series of books is by far the most concise and fun to work with when helping kids. Adults also enjoy them.

C J Gascoine

Very thorough and approachable theory practice book for young students age 7 upwards.

Susan A. Harris

Theory can be a barrier for some young students but this book is set out well, it's easy to read and understand, and has logical progression. Highly recommended.

Steve Riches

I might at last be able to learn my theory and I am an old age pensioner learning to play the piano.

Violet

Very good book that puts things very simply. I was recommended this by my piano teacher even though I am an adult learner as it covers all the technical points very progressively.

Amazon Customer

Music Theory is Fun Book 1

978-1-987926-09-5

Treble clef, bass clef, notes and letter names. Time names and values. Dotted notes, tied notes and rests. Accidentals, tones and semitones. Key signatures and scales (C, G, D & F major). Degrees of the scale, intervals and tonic triads. Time signatures and bar-lines. Writing music and answering rhythms. Puzzles, quizzes and ten one-page tests. Musical terms dictionary and list of signs.

Music Theory is Fun Book 2

978-1-987926-10-1

Major key signatures to 3 sharps & flats. Minor keys to 1 sharp & flat. Degrees of the scale and intervals. Tonic triads. Keyboard, tones and semitones. Time signatures. Grouping notes and rests, triplets. Two ledger lines below and above the staves. Writing four-bar rhythms. Puzzles, quizzes and ten one-page tests. Musical terms and signs.

Music Theory is Fun Book 3

978-1-987926-11-8

Major & minor key signatures 4 sharps or flats. Harmonic and melodic minor scales. Degrees of the scale, intervals, tonic triads. Simple and compound time signatures. Grouping notes & rests. Transposition at the octave. More than two ledger lines. Writing four-bar rhythms, anacrusis. Phrases. Puzzles, quizzes and ten one-page tests. Musical terms & signs.

Music Theory is Fun Book 4

978-1-987926-12-5

Key signatures to 5 sharps or flats. Alto clef. Chromatic scale, double sharps & flats. Technical names of notes in the diatonic scale. Simple & compound time, duple, triple, quadruple. Primary triads, tonic, subdominant & dominant. Diatonic intervals up to an octave. Ornaments. Four-bar rhythms and rhythms to words. Orchestral instruments and their clefs. Puzzles, quizzes and ten one-page tests. Musical terms & signs including French.

Music Theory is Fun Book 5

978-1-987926-13-2

Key signatures to 7 sharps or flats. Tenor clef and scales. Compound intervals: major, minor, perfect, diminished & augmented. Irregular time signatures, quintuple & septuple. Tonic, super-tonic, subdominant & dominant chords. Writing at concert pitch. Short & open score. Orchestral instruments. Composing a melody. Perfect, imperfect & plagal cadences. Puzzles, quizzes and ten one-page tests. Musical terms and signs including French and German.

Music Theory is Fun – A Handy Reference

978-1-987926-14-9

A concise reference to all the rudiments of music covered by the above five Music Theory is Fun books.

MUSIC THEORY IS FUN
BOOK 1

Maureen Cox

All enquiries regarding this paperback edition to:

Mimast Inc
email: mimast.inc@gmail.com

For my granddaughter Flora

* * * * * *

If you want to play an instrument, sing well or just improve your listening, you need to read music and understand theory.

This book takes you through the theory of music in a simple, straightforward way. There are plenty of fun illustrations and a variety of activities to help you along.

Towards the back of the book there are puzzles, quizzes and ten one-page tests composed of questions you could meet in an exam. At the end of the book there is a dictionary of musical terms and a list of signs for easy reference

With my help you can take your first steps on the road to mastering and enjoying the theory of music. With this book you can discover that Theory is Fun.

Maureen Cox

Acknowledgements

I am grateful to the many Professional Private Music Teachers and Members of the Incorporated Society of Musicians who used Theory is Fun with their pupils and to Christina Bourne, Brenda Harris, Alison Hogg, Judith Holmes, Ann Leggett and Marion Martin for their helpful suggestions. I am especially grateful to Alison Hounsome for her insightful comments and helpful recommendations in the preparation of this revised edition.

A word about this revised edition

Using the previous editions of my Theory is Fun books, more than a half million people, young and not so young, mostly in the UK, had fun learning music theory. This edition has been revised and extended to include students in other countries such as America and Canada where, for example, a bar is a measure, a minim is a half note and a tone is a whole step. Common alternatives terms are listed at the back of the book with a dictionary of musical terms and signs.

This book covers the basic rudiments of theory required by the various Boards and Colleges including the Associated Board of the Royal Schools of Music, Trinity College London, the Music Examinations Boards of Australia and New Zealand and the Royal Conservatory of Canada.

Any errors are entirely my responsibility. Should there be any in this edition, I would be most grateful for them to be drawn to my attention so that they may be corrected in a future edition.

Maureen Cox

CONTENTS

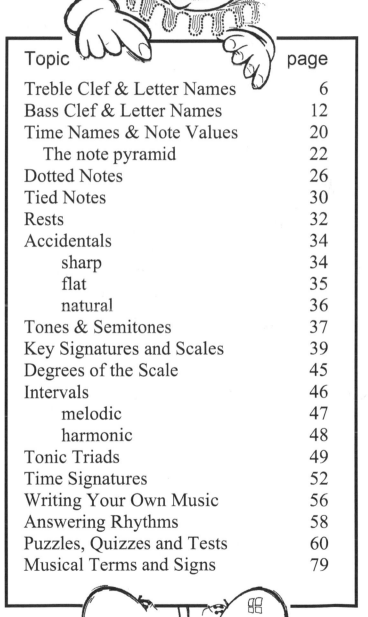

The G g clef   Go to 19,

THE TREBLE CLEF

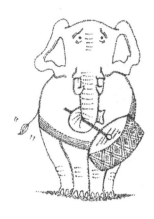

This is a treble clef.

Can you finish these treble clefs?

G

Now you draw four treble clefs.

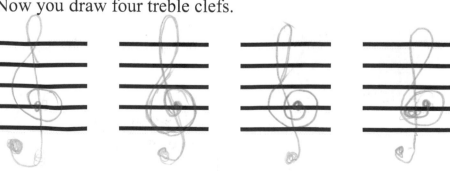

LETTER NAMES

The notes **E G B D F** sit on the lines.

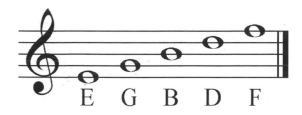

E   G   B   D   F

Elephant **G**eorge **B**eats **D**rum **F**ast

Every Good Boy Deserves Fish
Fun
Football

The notes **F A C E** sit in the spaces.

F   A   C   E

Think of a happy face and you will
remember the notes **F A C E**

Test yourself

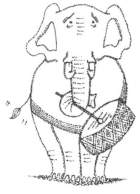

Show Elephant George how well you know the notes in the treble clef.

Write the letter name on the line under the note. Remember the happy face.

Count how many you had right.
Put the number in the box.

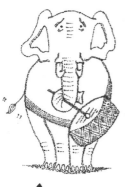

Draw the note ⬮ on a line or in a
space to match the letter name.

Each of these nine notes is in a
different place on the stave.

F

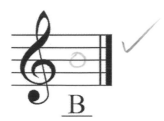
B

D

F

G

E

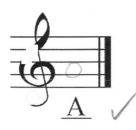
A

C

E

Count how many you had right.
Put the number in the box.

8/9

9

The lost puppy

Fill in the letter names of the notes.

Tom looked into the water.

He saw his F A C E
looking back at him.

Suddenly he saw another F A C E
next to his.

It was a puppy.
It looked lost.

"I wonder what A G E it is?" thought Tom.

10

The puppy looked hungry.

Tom had a biscuit in his pocket.

Should he F E E D it?

Then Tom saw a boy. He was calling,

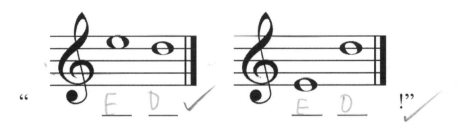

" E D ✓ E D !" ✓

Tom was happy. The puppy was not lost any more.

THE BASS CLEF

. bass clef

Draw a bass clef in each space.

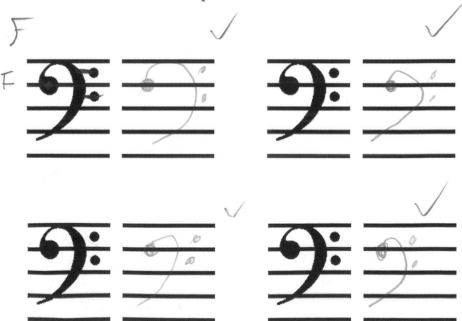

LETTER NAMES

The notes **G B D F A** sit on the lines.

G   B   D   F   A

Georgina **B**ear **D**eserves **F**ood **A**lways.

Good   Boys Deserves Fudge Always.

The notes **A   C   E   G** sit in the spaces.

A   C   E   G

All **C**ats **E**njoy **G**rieg

Grass

Test yourself

Show Georgina Bear how well you know the bass clef notes. Name each of the nine notes.

Put the number in the box to show how many you had right.

Draw the note ⵔ on a line or in a space to match the letter name.

Each of these nine notes is in a different place on the stave.

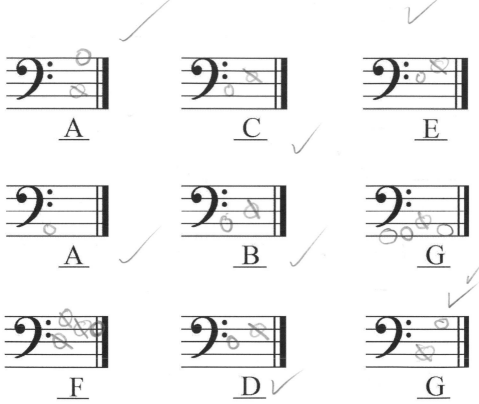

A   C   E

A   B   G

F   D   G

Count how many you had right. Put the number in the box.

Life on the farm

Fill in the letter names of the notes.

Early one morning a farmer

took a _B_ _A_ _G_ of corn

and set out to

_F_ _E_ _E_ _D_ the chickens.

They were pleased to see him.

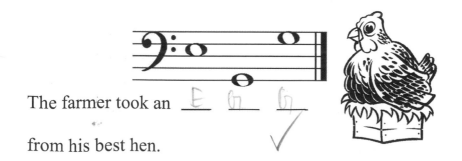

The farmer took an _E_ _G_ _G_

from his best hen.

16

He showed it to his son A B E

who was in the cowshed milking the cows.

"What a fine E G G ,"

said A B E .

Then the farmer went to the field to

look at a C A B B A G E

to see if it was ready to cut for dinner.

More notes

There are notes on the lines and in the spaces of the **stave** or **staff**. There are other notes that sit on top and underneath.

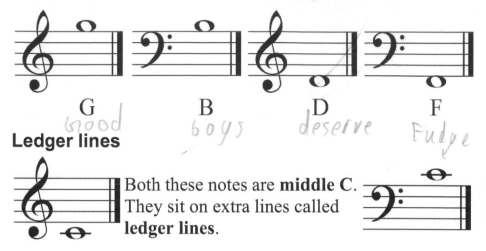

G   B   D   F

Good   *boys*   *deserve*   *Fudge*

Ledger lines

Both these notes are **middle C**. They sit on extra lines called **ledger lines**.

Test yourself

Put a treble clef or a bass clef in front of each note to make it say its correct name.

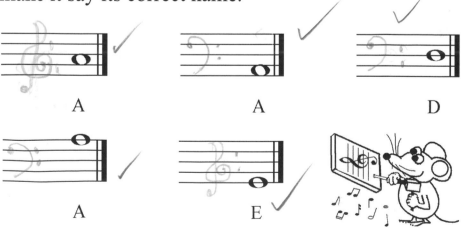

A   A   D

A   E

Count how many you had right.
Put the number in the box.

15 / 15

TIME NAMES & NOTE VALUES

You now know the names of all the notes and where they are on the **stave** or **staff**.

Common 4/4

So far you have met only the **letter** names of the notes.

Notes also have **time** names.

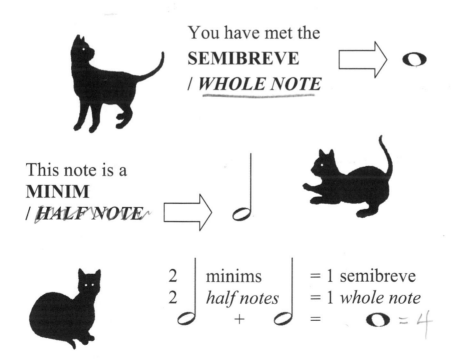

You have met the
SEMIBREVE
/ WHOLE NOTE ⟹ 𝅝

This note is a
MINIM
/ HALF NOTE ⟹ 𝅗𝅥

2	minims	= 1 semibreve
2	*half notes*	= 1 *whole note*

𝅗𝅥 + 𝅗𝅥 = 𝅝 = 4

This note is a
CROTCHET
/ *QUARTER NOTE*

2	crotchets	= 1	minim
2	*quarter notes*	= 1	*half note*

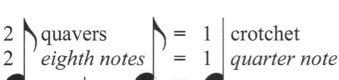

This note is a
QUAVER
/ *EIGHTH NOTE*

2	quavers	= 1	crotchet
2	*eighth notes*	= 1	*quarter note*

This note is a
SEMIQUAVER
/ *SIXTEENTH NOTE*

2	semiquavers	= 1	quaver
2	*sixteenth notes*	= 1	*eighth note*

Notes worth less than a crotchet / *quarter note* can be joined together or **beamed**.

 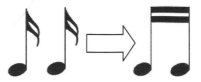

21

The note pyramid

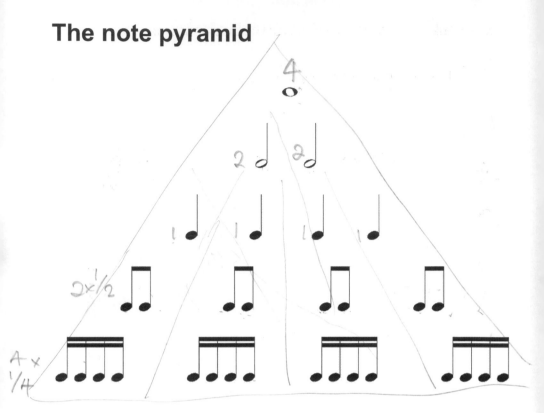

The note pyramid is very useful. You can see at a glance the values of the notes.

For example, you can see that a semibreve / ~~whole note~~ is worth two minims / ~~half notes~~ or sixteen semiquavers / ~~sixteenth notes~~.

Use the **note pyramid** to find the correct number.

A semibreve / ~~whole note~~ equals

2	minims / ~~half notes~~ ✓
4	crotchets / ~~quarter notes~~ ✓
~~4~~8	quavers / ~~eighth notes~~ ✓
16	semiquavers / ~~sixteenth notes~~ ✓

A minim / ~~half note~~ equals

2	crotchets / *quarter notes* ✓
4	quavers / *eighth notes* ✓
8	semiquavers / *sixteenth notes* ✓

A crotchet / *quarter note* equals

| 2 | ✓ quavers / *eighth notes* |
| 4 | ✓ semiquavers / *sixteenth notes* |

A quaver / *eighth note* equals

| 2 | ✓ semiquavers / *sixteenth notes* |

Test your note values

How many

crotchets / *quarter notes* in a semibreve / *whole note*? 4

semiquavers / *sixteenth* notes in a quaver / *eighth note*? 2

quavers / *eighth notes* or in a crotchet / *quarter note*? 4

minims / *half notes* in a semibreve / *whole note*? 2 ✓

semiquavers / *sixteenth notes* in a crotchet / *quarter* note? 4

quavers / *eighth notes* in a minim / *half note*? 4 ✓

crotchets / *quarter notes* in a minim / *half note*? 2 ✓

quavers / *eighth notes* in a semibreve / *whole note*? 8 ✓

semiquavers / *sixteenth notes* in a minim / *half note*? 8 ✓

semiquavers / *sixteenth notes* in a semibreve / *whole note*? 16

How many did you get right?
Put the number in the box.

10

Where shall I put the stem?

The stems of notes are on the **left** when they go **down**.  = Pizza

 The stems are on the **right** when they go **up**.

If a note is written **above** the **middle line**, its stem goes **down**.

d = for doughnut

When a note is written **below** the **middle line**, its stem goes **up**.

If a note is written **on** the **middle line**, its stem can go **up** but often it goes **down**.

Draw stems for **crotchets / *quarter notes*** in the treble clef.

 Stave

Draw stems for **quavers / *eighth notes*** in the bass clef..

DOTTED NOTES

A dot after a note is worth **half** the value of the note.

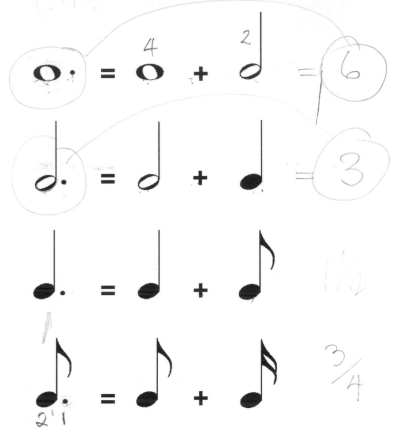

A dot is placed in the **same space**
if a dotted note is **in a space**.

A dot is placed in the **space above**
if a dotted note is **on a line**.

26

Test yourself

Fill in the missing numbers.

 4

♪. = | 3 | semiquavers *sixteenth notes* ✓

♩. = | 3 | quavers *eighth notes*

𝅝 = | 4 | crotchets *quarter notes* ✓

♩. = | 3 | crotchets *quarter notes*

𝅗𝅥 = | 4 | quavers *eighth notes*

♪. = | 3 | quavers *eighth notes*

𝅝. = | 3 | minims *half notes*

𝅝 = | 8 | quavers *eighth notes*

Draw one note for your answer.

♩. + ♪ = ___ 𝅗𝅥

1½ + ½

𝅗𝅥 + 𝅗𝅥 + 𝅗𝅥 = 𝅝.

How many did you get right?
Put the number in the box.

| 10 |
| 10 |

Test yourself

Draw

(1) a semibreve / *whole note* in each space of the stave.

(2) a crotchet / *quarter note* on each line of the stave.

(3) a minim / *half note* in each space of the stave.

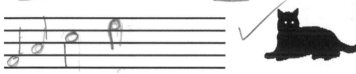

(4) a quaver / *eighth note* on each line of the stave.
The 'tail' is on the right-hand side of the stem.

(5) a minim / *half note* on middle C.

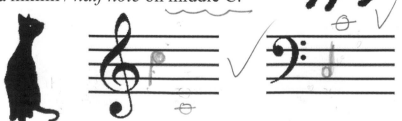

28

(6) a semiquaver / *sixteenth note* in each space of the stave.

 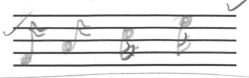

(7) two quavers / *eighth notes* joined together
in the C space.

pizza

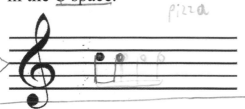 

(8) two semiquavers / *sixteenth notes* joined together
on the G line.

Good Boys Deserve Fun Always

A
F
D
B
G

(9) a dotted minim / *dotted half note* in each space.

 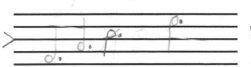

(10) a dotted crotchet / *dotted quarter note* on each line.

TIED NOTES

A tie joins notes which are **at the same pitch**. The notes sound the same.

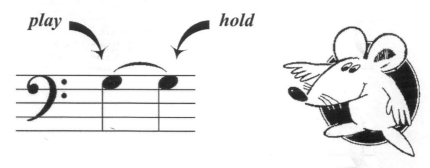

Tied notes are joined together **at the heads** (not the stems) and **from the outside** (not the inside) of each head.

You can join more than two notes with ties as long as they are the **same notes** and are **next to each other**.

30

Count the beats

How many crotchets / ~~quarter notes~~ is each tie worth?

How many answers did you have right?
Put the number in the box.

RESTS

crotchet

There are times in music when we need to be absolutely quiet. In order to do this, we use **rests** instead of notes.

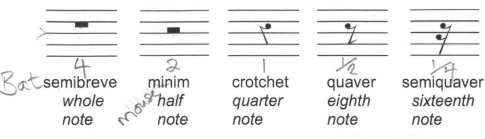

Bat

semibreve	minim	crotchet	quaver	semiquaver
whole note	*half note*	*quarter note*	*eighth note*	*sixteenth note*

mouse

If you want to rest for the length of a **dotted** note, put a **dot** after the rest in the **second space from the top** of the stave.

Now put the correct **rest** to match each note:-

There are two ways to write a **crotchet / _quarter note_** rest.
The one you have met so far is the easiest, but the one below
is very impressive if you can copy it accurately.

It looks like a **c** with a **z** on top.

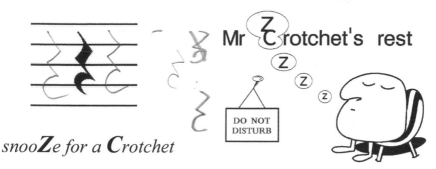

Mr Crotchet's rest

DO NOT
DISTURB

snoo$Z$_e for a_ C_rotchet_

Try to match the rests

with these notes **without** looking back at the last page:-

How many were correct?
Put the number in the box.

ACCIDENTALS

I expect you have noticed in your music that there are sometimes signs in front of notes. These signs are called **accidentals**. There are three accidentals - the sharp, the flat and the natural.

The sharp

It looks like this.

= (Hashtag)

It is written **in front** of a note and makes that note **higher**.

D#

Write a sharp **in front** of each crotchet / *quarter note*.

The flat

It looks like a small letter b.

It is written **in front** of a note and makes that note **lower**.

Write a flat ♭ **in front** of each minim / *half note*.

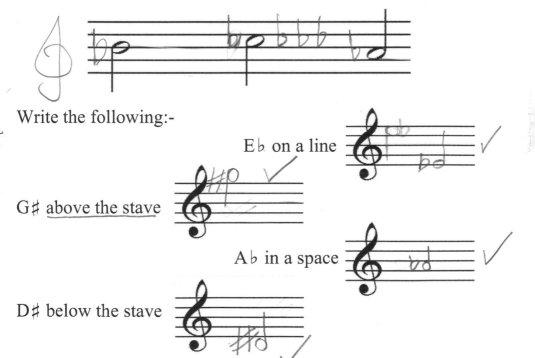

Write the following:-

E♭ on a line

G♯ above the stave

A♭ in a space

D♯ below the stave

The Natural = normal

It looks like this.

It is written **in front** of a note that has been raised or lowered and it changes the note back to its normal pitch.

This means it can make a note **higher** or **lower**.

If you have an accidental in a bar / ~~measure~~ of music, it changes all other notes in the bar / ~~measure~~ which are at the same pitch.

If a note is an octave higher or lower, you will need another accidental if you want to raise or lower it.

Important
Accidentals are written **in front** of notes.

TONES AND SEMITONES

The easiest way to learn about tones / *steps* and semitones / *half steps* is to study closely a piano keyboard.

First of all, learn the names of the **white** keys. There are only seven: **ABCDEFG**. Then look at the **black** keys: they come between some of the white keys.

When you move **up the keyboard** the black keys are called **sharps**.

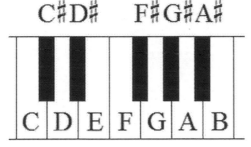

When you move **down the keyboard** the black keys are called **flats**.

B & C and E & F have no black key between them. This means that there is a **semitone** / *half step* between B & C and E & F.

semitones / *half steps*

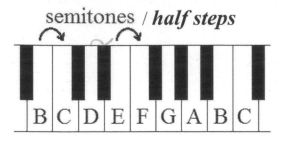

Every step you take between a **black** key and a **white** key is a **semitone** / *half step*. You take **two semitones** / *half steps* for a **tone** / *whole step*.

2 semitones / *2 half steps* = 1 tone / *1 whole step*

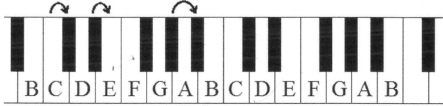

Black keys can be sharps or flats.

Fill in the missing letter names:

D raised one semitone / ~~half step~~ = D♯

B lowered one semitone / ~~half step~~ = B♭

C raised one tone / ~~whole step~~ = D

F lowered one tone / ~~whole step~~ = E♭

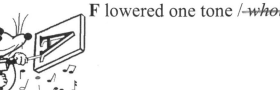

4

KEY SIGNATURES AND SCALES

Here are four important key signatures. They tell you which accidentals are in the scale.

C major   G major   D major   F major

Funny Enij has 1. Flat

Important

Notice where the accidentals are written on the stave. They are **always** on these lines and spaces when they are written as key signatures.

C Major has no sharps and no flats.

G Major has one sharp – F

D Major has two sharps - F and C.

Think of **F**ather **C**hristmas and you will always remember the order of sharps.

F Major has one flat - B.

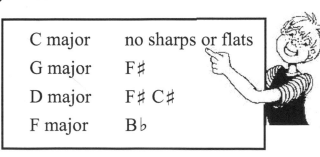

C major	no sharps or flats
G major	F♯
D major	F♯ C♯
F major	B♭

Now you have met four key signatures, you are ready to learn about their scales. A **scale** is a group of notes arranged in order. For example, in C major, the order is **C D E F G A B C**.

C Major

There are no accidentals in C major which makes it very easy.

Here is the scale in semibreves / *whole notes* **ascending** – going up. Write the names of the eight notes.

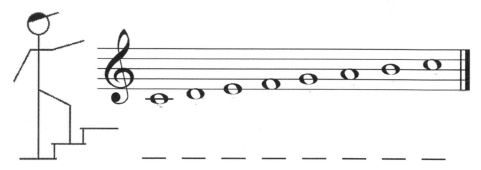

Here is the scale in semibreves / *whole notes* **descending** – going down. Write the names of the eight notes.

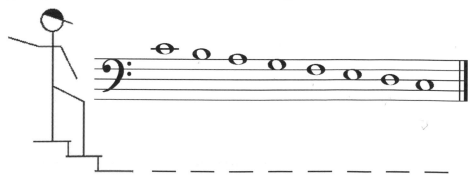

In **all major** scales there is a **semitone** / *half step* between notes 3-4 and 7-8.

This is how you can mark semitones / *half steps*.

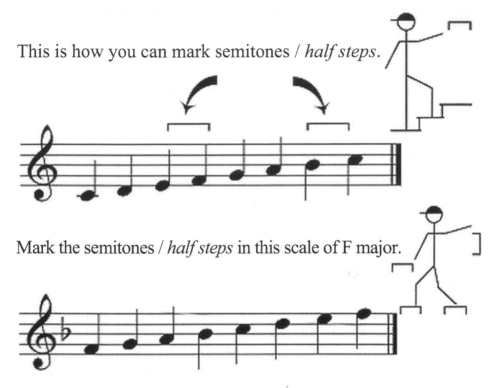

Mark the semitones / *half steps* in this scale of F major.

Important
When descending, you can find the semitones / *half steps* by counting from the bottom of the scale.

8 7 6 5 4 3 2 1

G Major

Write the key signatures in the correct places in the treble and bass clefs.

①

When, for example, you are asked to write the scale of G Major ascending, without key signature, in crotchets / quarter notes in the treble clef, marking the semitones / half steps, it is a good idea to **underline all the important instructions first**.

I did this one for you. ☺

Write the scale of G Major ascending, in crotchets / quarter notes, with key signature, in the bass clef.

Mark the semitones / half steps with ⌐⌐.

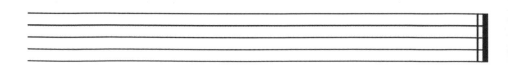

D Major

Write the key signatures in the correct places in the treble and bass clefs. Clue:- **Father Christmas.**

Write the scale of <u>D Major</u> <u>descending</u>, in <u>crotchets</u> / *quarter notes*, <u>with</u> key signature, in the <u>treble clef</u>.

Mark the <u>semitones</u> / *half steps* like this ⌐¬ . ☺

☺ I did this one for you as well.

Write the scale of D Major ascending, in crotchets / *quarter notes*, without key signature, in the treble clef.

Draw ⌐¬ over each semitone / *half step*.

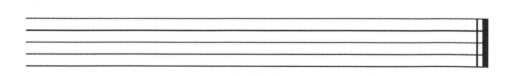

F Major

Write the key signatures in the correct places in the treble and bass clefs.

Underline the important words in this question:

Write the scale of F Major ascending, without key signature, in minims / *half notes*, in the bass clef. Mark the semitones / *half steps*.

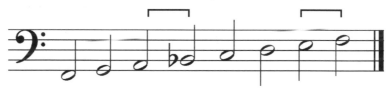

Underline the important words in this question. Remember to use ⌐‾⌐ to mark the semitones / *half steps*.

Write the scale of F Major descending, in minims / *half notes*, with key signature, in the treble clef.

Mark the semitones / *half steps*.

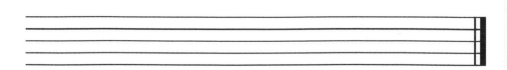

DEGREES OF THE SCALE

The first note of the scale is called the keynote or the **first degree**. Therefore the second note is the **2nd degree**, the third, the **3rd degree** and so on, until you reach the **8th degree** or **octave** - written as **8ve**.

Write the degree of the scale which is asked for.

I have written the first answer for you. ☺

3rd   1st   8ve   4th

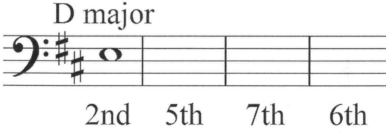

2nd   5th   7th   6th

How many did you get right?
Put the number in the box.

6

INTERVALS

An interval is the **distance** or **difference in pitch between two notes**.

For example, in D major there is an interval of a 3rd (third) between notes D and F♯.

I have written the scale of D major to show you each interval.

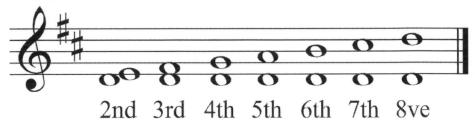

2nd 3rd 4th 5th 6th 7th 8ve

Write the intervals for G major in the same way.

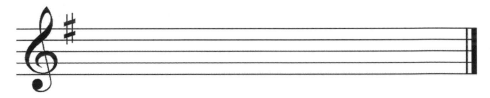

Write the key signature and the intervals for F major.

The melodic interval

This is a melodic interval.

When the two notes are written **one after the other** they are **played separately**.

Put a number below the stave to show which melodic interval has been written. I have answered the first one for you. ☺

4th ___   ___   ___

___   ___   ___   ___

How many did you get right?
Put the number in the box

7

The harmonic interval

This interval is a harmonic interval.

When the two notes are written **one above the other** they are
played at the same time.

Write a note above each of the keynotes to make the
harmonic interval. I have written the first one for you.

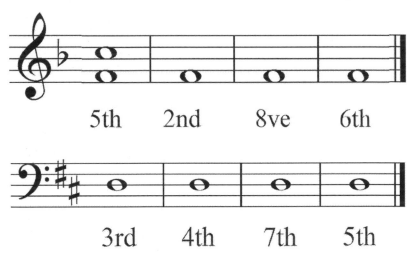

5th   2nd   8ve   6th

3rd   4th   7th   5th

How many did you get right?
Put the number in
the box.

7

Important
Remember, we always count from the keynote.

TONIC TRIADS

The first note of a scale is called the **keynote** or the **tonic**. A tonic triad is made up of **three** notes:-

1. The keynote or tonic.

2. The 3rd degree (note) of the scale.

3. The 5th degree (note) of the scale.

Sometimes you will be asked to write a tonic triad **with** key signature.

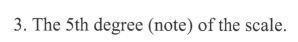

Sometimes you will be asked to write a tonic triad **without** key signature. This will only be a problem in D Major where the 3rd note is F sharp.

Test yourself

Write these tonic triads **with** key signature

G major

F major

Write these tonic triads **without** key signature

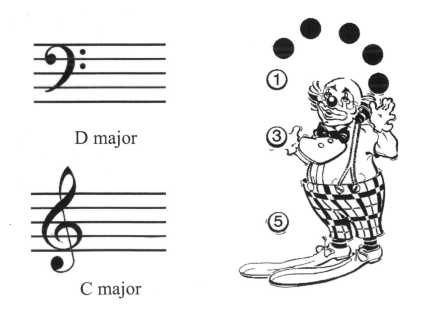

D major

C major

Draw the **treble clef** and these tonic triads
with key signature.

F major	G major	D major

Draw the **bass clef** and these tonic triads
with key signature.

G major	D major	F major

Draw the **treble clef** and these tonic triads
without key signature.

F major	D major	G major

Draw the **bass clef** and these tonic triads
without kcy signature.

G major	D major	C major

How many were correct?
Put the number in the box.

16

TIME SIGNATURES

At the beginning of a piece of music you will find a **Clef**, a **Key** signature of sharps or flats (but not for C major) and **two numbers** we call a **Time** signature.

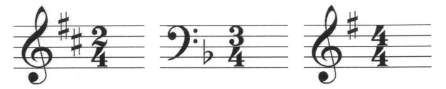

The order is always the same and you can remember it because the words are in alphabetical order:-

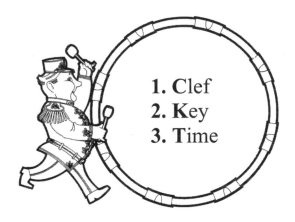

1. Clef
2. Key
3. Time

The **top number** of the time signature tells you **how many** beats there are in a bar / *measure*.

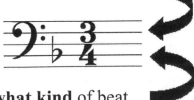

The **bottom number** tells you **what kind** of beat.

Simple duple time

In this book you will meet only one simple **duple** time signature. Duple means two.

Duple time is $\frac{2}{4}$.

The top number [**2**] tells us there are two beats in a bar / *measure.*
The bottom number [**4**] tells us the beats are crotchets / *quarter notes.*

Bar lines divide music into **bars / *measures.***

A double bar line comes at the end of a piece of music. It is written as a thin line followed by a thicker line.

Here is a passage of music in $\frac{2}{4}$ time.

I have left out **two bar lines**. Put them in for me.

What is the name of the key of the passage? ____ major.

Simple triple time

In this book you will only meet one simple **triple** time signature. Triple means three.

Triple time is $\frac{3}{4}$.

The top number [**3**] tells us there are

_____.

The bottom number [**4**] tells us

_____.

What does the time signature $\frac{3}{4}$ means. Write your answer here.

_____

Simple quadruple time

In this book you will only meet one simple **quadruple** time signature. Quadruple means four.

Quadruple time is $\frac{4}{4}$.

$\frac{4}{4}$ is sometimes written as **C**.

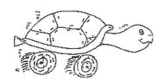

Write down what $\frac{4}{4}$ or **C** means here.

_____

Test yourself on time signatures

Add **one note** to each bar / *measure* (under the ∗) so that the time signature is correct.

Test yourself on bar lines

Add the missing bar lines.

WRITING RHYTHMS

In $\frac{2}{4}$ time.

If there are semiquavers / *sixteenth notes* beam them together in crotchet / *quarter note* beats. Join the tails or flags. Do this with any group that has a semiquaver / *sixteenth note*.

Notice we use a **semibreve / *whole note* rest** (*) for a whole bar or measure.

In $\frac{3}{4}$ time.

You can beam together a whole bar of quavers / *eighth notes*.

In $\frac{4}{4}$ time.

You can join beats 1 and 2 or 3 and 4.

You **cannot** join beats 2 and 3 using **beamed** notes.

You know all the notes and rests. You have seen examples of rhythms in simple time. You know all the rules. Well, now it's your turn!

In the space for the note A, write **four** bars / *measures* of rhythms, with time signature, in each of these given times.

simple **duple** time:

simple **triple** time:

simple **quadruple** time

simple **triple** time:

ANSWERING RHYTHMS

In an exam you could be given a two-bar rhythm with a time signature and asked to write another two bars.

Hints

Tap the rhythm to yourself and feel how it should continue and how it should end. It would not feel right to end on a very short note such as a semiquaver / *sixteenth note*.

Here is a two-bar rhythm:

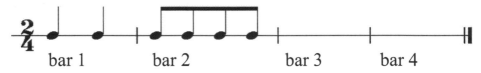

bar 1   bar 2   bar 3   bar 4

You may want to use one of the rhythms given in bars one or two.   That is fine as long as you put some rhythms of your own to show that you understand how to write music.

There is not one correct answer but many. Bars 1 and 3 could have the same rhythm:

or bars 2 and 3 could have the same rhythm:

Write two-bar answering rhythms for the following:

ta-ra-ra   boom-de-ay

PUZZLES

QUIZZES

TESTS

Fun page

Connect the note to the rest of the same length.

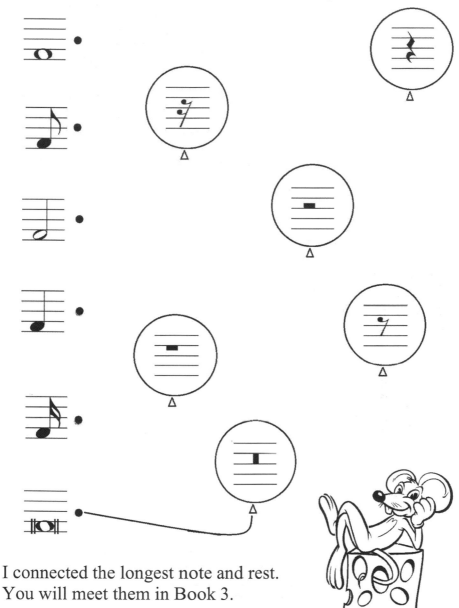

I connected the longest note and rest.
You will meet them in Book 3.

Merry-go-round

The last letter or the last two letters of one word will be the start of the next word. Go around the shell to find the answers to the questions below.

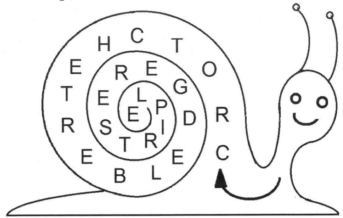

This is a _____ / *quarter note.*

This is the called the _____ clef.

These notes are on _____ lines.

This is called a _____ .

This is indicates simple _____ time.

Word search

E	B	A	N	D	A	N	T	E	D
O	L	O	D	E	N	I	F	E	O
A	E	L	P	A	N	V	E	L	T
O	G	C	K	L	G	V	C	O	A
C	A	N	T	A	B	I	L	E	C
P	T	M	A	R	L	V	O	X	C
T	O	B	H	G	I	A	D	O	A
P	I	A	N	O	U	C	E	T	T
N	A	S	O	I	J	E	M	I	S
D	R	A	X	P	O	C	O	S	S

Meaning	Musical term
A little	poco
At a walking pace	
Slow, stately, broad	
Soft	
The end	
Smoothly	
In a singing style	
Slow, leisurely	
Lively, quick	
Sweetly	
Short, detached	

63

Crossword

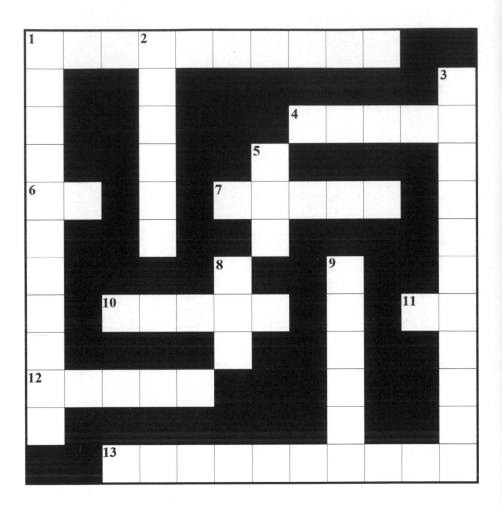

Clues

Across

1 gradually slower

4 loud

6 3rd and 4th degree of C major

7 speed, time

10 slow and stately, broad

11 6th and 7th degrees of D major

12 sweetly

13 gradually softer

Down

1 becoming gradually slower

2 slow, leisurely

3 gradually softer

5 tonic triad

8 1st, 2nd and 3rd degrees in the scale of F major

9 lively, quick

Answers?

Yes. Ready to check?

Quiz 1

Put a tick / *check mark* (✓) in the correct box.

1. adagio

☐ at a walking pace

☐ slow, leisurely

☐ lively, reasonably fast

☐ slightly slower than allegro

2. staccato

☐ suddenly

☐ smoothly

☐ very quick

☐ short, detached

3. sweetly

☐ cantabile

☐ dolce

☐ maestoso

☐ pesante

4. quietly

☐ forte

☐ leggiero

☐ piano

☐ tranquillo

5. scherzo

☐ a joke

☐ lightly

☐ heavily

☐ playfully

6. gradually softer

☐ decresc.

☐ rall.

☐ rit.

☐ *sfz*

Check your answers.
Put a number in the box. ☐ / 6

66

Quiz 2

Put a tick / *check mark* (✓) in the correct box.

1. ▷

☐ becoming louder

☐ becoming softer

☐ accent the note

☐ slur

2. >

☐ becoming softer

☐ accent the note

☐ pause on the note

☐ short, detached

3. ◁

☐ becoming softer

☐ becoming louder

☐ becoming slower

☐ short, detached

4. ⌢• ⌣•

☐ short, detached

☐ accent the note

☐ play an octave higher

☐ pause on the note

5. **play notes smoothly**

☐ 8va ⌐‾‾‾‾¬
   8 - - - - - - -

☐ ◁▷

☐ ⌒

☐ ⌢• ⌣•

6. **gradually louder**

☐ *sfz*

☐ **cresc.**

☐ **rall.**

☐ **rit**

Check your answers. Put a number in the box.

☐ / 6

Handy hints for tests

This section is for you to practise the different types of questions you could have in a test or an exam.

The questions could be on any topic covered in this book.

Revise each topic in this book thoroughly.

Don't forget to study musical terms and signs – they are **always** included.

Practice
makes perfect !

Practice
makes perfect !

If you have worked through this book carefully and understood each topic, this will be an easy task for you.

Before you begin any test, write out your key signature chart from page 39. Always refer to the chart when tackling questions that require you to know a key signature.

Test 1

Put a tick / *check mark* (✓) in the correct box.

1. Name this note:

   A ☐   D ☐   B ☐

2. Name this note:

   B natural ☐   G flat ☐   B flat ☐

3. Name the notes to find the hidden word:

   CAFE ☐   CAGE ☐   FACE ☐

4. How many quavers / *eighth notes* are there in a minim / *half note*?

   2 ☐   4 ☐   8 ☐

5. For how many crotchets / *quarter notes* does this rest last?

   3 ☐   2 ☐   4 ☐

6. Which is the correct time signature?

   $\frac{3}{4}$ ☐ $\frac{4}{4}$ ☐ $\frac{2}{4}$ ☐

Test 2

1. Which pair of notes has a distance / *step* of a semitone / *half step* between them?

A and B ☐ F and G ☐ B and C ☐

2. Here is the scale of F major. Where are the semitones / *half steps*?

1 2 3 4 5 6 7 8

Between 1st and 2nd and 7th and 8th degrees ☐
Between 3rd and 4th and 7th and 8th degrees ☐
Between 5th and 6th and 7th and 8th degrees ☐

3. Which is the correct key signature of D major?

4. Choose the key note for this tonic triad.

F ☐   G ☐   C ☐

5. Which note needs to be added to complete this tonic triad in G major?

C ☐   B ☐   A ☐

6. Name this interval.

5th ☐   7th ☐   6th ☐

70

Test 3

Write the words.

1. 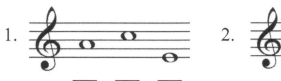 _ _ _

2. 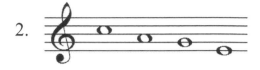 _ _ _ _

3.  _ _ _ _

4.  _ _ _ _

5.  _ _ _

6.  _ _ _ _

7. 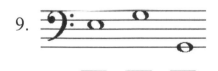 _ _ _

8. 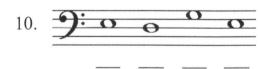 _ _ _

9. 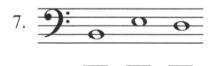 _ _ _ _

10.  _ _ _ _

11.  _ _ _ _

12.  _ _ _ _

Test 4

Write the notes.

1.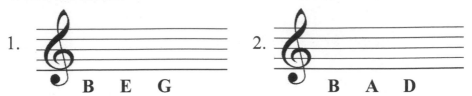
   B   E   G   2. B   A   D

3.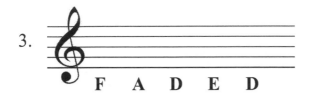
   F   A   D   E   D

4.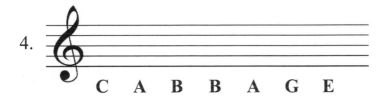
   C   A   B   B   A   G   E

5.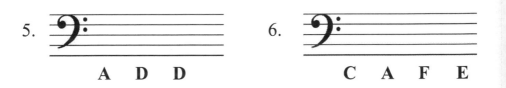
   A   D   D   6. C   A   F   E

7.
   B   E   G   G   E   D

8.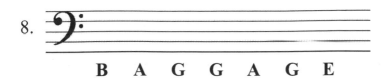
   B   A   G   G   A   G   E

Test 5

1. 2 crotchets / *quarter notes* = 1 _____ / _____

2. 2 semiquavers / *sixteenth notes* = 1 _____ / _____

3. 2 quavers / *eighth notes* = 1 _____ / _____

4. 1 minim / *half note* = ___ quavers / *eighth notes*.

5. 1 semibreve / *whole note* = ___ minims / *half notes*.

6. 1 crotchet / *quarter note* = ___ semiquavers / *sixteenth notes*.

7. In $\frac{4}{4}$ time you can beam together beats __&__ and __&__

8. In $\frac{4}{4}$ time you cannot beam together beats __&__ and __&__

9. $\frac{3}{4}$ is simple _____ time.

10. $\frac{2}{4}$ is simple _____ time.

11. Write a whole bar of quavers / *eighth notes*.

$\frac{3}{4}$

12. Write a whole bar of quavers / *eighth notes*.

$\frac{4}{4}$

Test 6

1. Write the scale of F major ascending, one octave only. Use semibreves / *whole notes*. Put in the key signature. Mark the semitones / *half steps* with a bracket ⌐¬ or ⌊⌋.

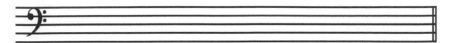

2. There are mistakes in the following music. Write it out correctly.

3. Answer the following rhythm.

4. Name the notes in the tonic triad of G major.

           GBD ☐   GBC ☐   GAD ☐

5. Name these intervals.

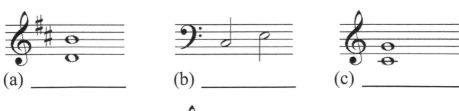

(a) _____   (b) _____   (c) _____

(d) _____   (e) _____   (f) _____

Test 7

1. Write a higher note above each given note to make the named harmonic interval. The first one has been done for you. The key is C major.

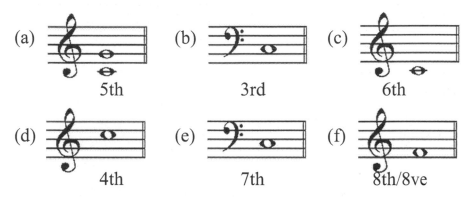

(a) 5th (b) 3rd (c) 6th

(d) 4th (e) 7th (f) 8th/8ve

2. Name the key of each scale. Draw a bracket over the notes that make a semitone / *half step*. The first one is done for you.

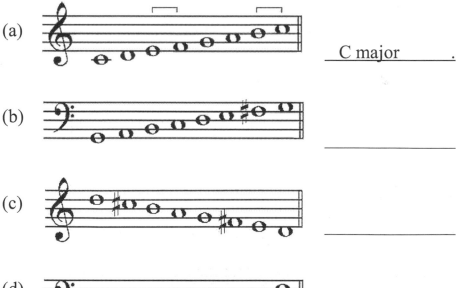

(a) _____C major_____.

(b) _____

(c) _____

(d) _____

Test 8

1. Name the degree of the scale of the notes marked * . The key is C major.

5th ___   ___   ___   ___   ___

2. Name the key of each tonic triad.

_____   _____   _____   _____

3. Write tonic triads with key signature for the following:

F major   G major   D major

4. Write these dynamics in the correct order from the quietest to the loudest.

f mp ff pp mf p

___   ___   ___   ___   ___   ___

5. Name the key of this scale _____
Mark the semitones / *half steps* with ⌐¬.

Test 9

Answer the questions on these eight bars / *measures*.

1. What is the major key of this music?

   _____

2. How many crotchets / *quarter notes* are in a bar / *measure*?

   _____

3. In which bar / *measure* is the rhythm the same as bar / *measure* 5?

   _____

4. Write the meaning of

   Presto _____

   mf _____

5. Which bars / *measures* have only staccato notes?

   _____

6. Write the highest and lowest notes as crotchets / *quarter notes*.

Test 10

1. Copy the piece of music above. Include the clef, key signature, time signature and all other details shown.

In this F major melody

2. What is the letter name of the highest note?_____

3. Name the degree of the scale in bar 2._____

4. Which bar / *measure* has all the notes of the tonic triad?___

5. How many staccato notes are there?_____

6. Answer true or false to this statement.
   The notes in bar / *measure* 5 are the quietest._____

7. Write the meaning of

   pp _____

   _____

8. What is the meaning of Andante?

   _____

9. Which bar / *measure* has a dotted crotchet / *dotted quarter note*? _____

MUSICAL TERMS AND SIGNS

Musical terms

A tempo - resume the normal speed

Accelerando - becoming gradually faster

Adagio - slow, leisurely

Allegro - lively, reasonably fast

Allegretto - slightly slower than allegro

Andante - at a walking pace

Andantino - a little slower or a little faster than Andante

Cantabile - in a singing style

Con - with

Crescendo [cresc.] - gradually louder

Da capo [D.C.] - from the beginning

Dal segno [D.S.] - repeat from the sign

Decrescendo [decresc.] - gradually softer

Diminuendo [dim.] - gradually softer

Dolce - sweetly

Fine - the end

Forte [*f*] - loud

Fortissimo [*ff*] - very loud

Forzando [*fz*] - with a strong accent

Largo - slow & stately, broad

Legato - smoothly

Leggiero - lightly

Lento - slowly

Maestoso - majestically

Mezzo forte [*mf*] - moderately loud

Mezzo piano [*mp*] - moderately soft

Moderato - at a moderate pace

Pesante - heavily

Piano [*p*] - soft

Pianissimo [*pp*] - very soft

Poco - a little

Presto - very quick

Prestissimo - as fast as possible

Rallentando [rall.] - becoming gradually slower

Ritardando [ritard. rit.] - gradually slower

Ritenuto [riten. rit.] - hold back, slower at once

Scherzo - a joke

Scherzando - playfully

Sforzando [*sf*, *sfz*] - with a sudden accent

Staccato - short, detached

Subito - suddenly

Tempo - speed, time

Tranquillo - quietly

Vivace - lively, quick

Common Alternative Terms

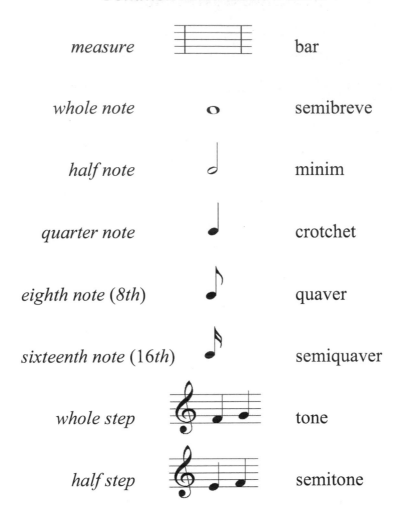

measure		bar
whole note		semibreve
half note		minim
quarter note		crotchet
eighth note (8th)		quaver
sixteenth note (16th)		semiquaver
whole step		tone
half step		semitone

Musical signs and symbols

 - accent the note

 - fermata: pause on the note

 - staccato: short, detached

- tie or bind same notes together

 - becoming louder

 - becoming softer

 - becoming louder then softer

 - start repeat and end repeat

 - slurs: play the group of notes smoothly

8va - - - - - - - - - ⌐ - play an octave higher

8vb - - - - - - - - ⌐ - play an octave lower

♭ ♮ ♯ - flat, natural and sharp

treble clef   bass clef

Printed in Great Britain
by Amazon